STEPPING
the Awk~

HOW TO HELP SOMEONE
WHO IS GRIEVING
THE DEATH OF A LOVED ONE

A Centering Corporation Resource
By Marilyn Gryte

Design by Janet Sieff, Centering Corporation
Edited by Andrea Gambill, *Grief Digest* Magazine

Library of Congress Cataloging-in-Publication Data

Gryte, Marilyn, 1949-
Stepping through the awkwardness : how to help someone who is grieving the death of a
loved one / by Marilyn Gryte.
    p. cm.
ISBN: 1-56123-138-X (alk paper)
    1. Grief. 2. Bereavement--Psychological aspects. 3. Death--Psychological aspects. 4.
Helping behavior. I. Title.

BF575.G7G79 2005
155.9'37--dc22

                                                                2005050180

www.centering.org

Dedication:

To each of you,
clients and patients,
who have shared with me your grief.
I looked for mentors and found them in you.

And to Ken,
whose love and nurturing warms my heart.

Table of Contents

Of Course We Feel Awkward

It is painful to be with those who grieve.

Their pain, whether it shows with tears, silence or anger, stirs our sense of helplessness. It's awkward to not know what to do or say. We're not sure what will be supportive to them. What will be invasive? We're embarrassed about our uncertainty. Somehow we presume we ought to know what to do when someone we care about is grieving.

When we feel helpless it's natural to want to flee or try to fix their grief, yet we squirm knowing neither is useful. Why do we feel so awkward?

Our awkwardness is understandable for at least three reasons.

1. **First, pain in others stirs our helplessness.** We are powerless to take their grief away, powerless to change what happened, powerless to make it not hurt. We like to see ourselves as competent. In the face of grief we are unsure, uneasy and less confident.

2. **Second, their grief reminds us of the losses we have had or may yet face in the future.** We see our own vulnerability. If this loss could happen to them, it could happen to us. It's scary to know we too could be in this much grief again.

3. **Third, few of us have had much classwork or modeling in what to do or say to a grieving person.** Keyboarding skills were required for high school graduation but skills in grief support were not. Adults around us may have been as anxious in the face of grief as we are and even professional training programs have often been abysmally lacking in providing guidance.

If you are reading this book, you want to know how to be more supportive to those who grieve. You are already on your way and we commend you. You are taking a big step from helplessness to helpfulness.

To ponder and discuss:

▶ What is hardest for me when I am with a grieving person?

▶ What is rewarding for me?

I was so afraid of saying the wrong thing and making it worse. Should I mention his daughter's death? Skip it? We worked at the same office, but I didn't know him well. I finally just said, "I'm thinking about Annette and I don't know if it helps or feels worse to have me say that."

"I want to know people remember her," he said quietly. *"It means a lot."*

Four Guiding Steps of Grief Support

The good news is that there are clear guidelines for how to be supportive to those who grieve. While every encounter is uniquely different, we do not need to be left in the dark. It will always be uncomfortable to see someone we care about in great pain, but it need not paralyze us.

Knowing how to begin helps lift the sense of helplessness.

With a map we can step into the unfamiliar with much more confidence and self-assurance.

Step One
LEARNING THE ART OF BEING RATHER THAN DOING

The primary role in grief support is to be a caring presence, and being present means being more aware of the person's grief than of our own discomfort. The most common obstacle to being fully present is our own sense of helplessness. Focusing on our helplessness compels us to do something—anything—to be more at ease again. We want to make their pain go away, or we want to get out of there. We scan for anything we can do or say to quiet their grief.

The first step is letting go of trying to fix their pain. We can't take away their pain. We can't give them back their loved one (or their health or their career or their marriage). It's not our job. Let it go. Allow the relief of not trying to do the impossible.

We cannot take anything away from their experience.

What we *can* do is imprint a memory of our caring beside their pain.

Think back to a time of loss or fear in your own life. Do you not also have a memory of someone's caring presence—their words, touch, or company—that is etched onto the painful memory? Perhaps there is a vacant place where you have always yearned for the memory of someone's caring.

The father who says, *Even the police officer gave me a hug* has the memory of caring etched onto the tragic story of his little boy's death while riding his bike. *The ultrasound technician had tears in her eyes when she squeezed my hand* is part of a woman's story when she tells of knowing her baby would be stillborn.

The memory of someone's caring is powerful. It's indelible. That's the kind of difference we can make. And that's a privilege. The art of *being with* means learning to wear our helplessness; to remember the saying, *When nothing helps—do nothing.* Breathe. Be. We are human beings, not human doings. There are things we can do in the name of grief support, but the doing is so much more useful when it is grounded in our being-ness and not instead of it.

Remember, your greatest gift is your caring presence.

Learn to recognize your own early signs of feeling helpless. Which is stronger, your urge to fix or to flee?

The sooner you recognize these signs the sooner you can quiet the automatic reactions and respond with a choice to be supportive.

We can set down our helplessness when we remember whose journey of healing it is. It is *their* pain and *their* journey.

Grief is a natural process.
When we have a physical wound our body is designed to heal.
When we have a grief wound we are also designed to heal.

Just as there are times when a wound becomes infected or a broken bone is out of alignment, there are times when grief becomes complicated and intervention is needed. But more often our role is to do as the seasoned OB doctor expressed it while sitting out a long tedious labor, *I need to keep my hands in my pockets.* The urge to intervene, to fix, to help can be strong and most of the time the process is natural—even if painfully slow.

- Our job is to be patient.
- Our job is to be present.
- Our job is to trust the healing process.

To ponder and discuss:

▸ What are my first signs that I'm beginning to feel helpless?

▸ What do I have the urge to do when I feel helpless?

▸ What do I need to remember to do when I feel helpless?

He was a student chaplain. He entered the hospital room of a terribly ill man and suddenly got queasy and dizzy at the sights and smells. Remembering his mother telling him, "If you feel faint, sit and put your head down low," he sat in the chair by the bed, head in his lap. He was embarrassed beyond words, recovered a bit, regrouped, touched the man's hand and then slipped out of the room. He had fled, and he felt a complete fool. It was two days before he had the courage to visit the man again. He walked in and could see the gentleman was much better. Before the chaplain could begin his speech of apology, the man said, "I want to tell you how meaningful it was to me that when I was so sick you came in and just sat by my bed and quietly prayed."

Step Two
Acknowledging the Obvious

One of our jobs is to avoid avoiding.
This means to acknowledge the obvious.
When we are uncomfortable, we easily avoid.

Grieving people tell volumes of stories of people turning away, ducking down a different aisle at the store, changing the subject when they mention their grief. And the only thing I hear grieving people complain about more than insensitive things said is when nothing at all is said about their loss.

People act as if nothing important has happened to me.
I'm angry. My pain seems to be invisible to others.

Mentioning their loss opens us to hearing their sadness and hurt. If tears flow, resist the fear that you have caused their pain. You haven't. You've just given them some company in their grief.

The first time you call on or happen to see someone after their loss may be your first step through the awkwardness for both of you. Letting them know three things may ease this meeting.

Let them know who you are.
Of course, this may be obvious and unnecessary. You may have known the person all your life. But if you don't see them often, it's best to just say your name.

Let them know what you know or just *that* you know.
People don't always know that you've heard of their loss. They may fear they need to break the news to you. *I read of your father's accident in the paper,* or *Our pastor told me about your daughter dying,* lets them know you are aware and how you heard.

Let them know you care.

I've been thinking of you.

I'm sorry this is such a difficult time for you.

These are simple ways to convey your caring. In just two or three sentences you can gently bridge the awkwardness of first encounters.

TO PONDER AND DISCUSS:

▸ What is a situation of a first meeting when I felt awkward?

▸ What might I do differently now?

▸ What does a grieving person need most from me?

▸ What gifts do I have to offer?

I was making one of my first home visits. It was to a mom after the stillbirth of her baby boy. I wondered what on earth I was supposed to say at a time like this. I had rehearsed a few phrases for openers. I knocked on the door and introduced myself. She welcomed me inside. I scrambled for the wise words I had imagined saying but they had vanished. My pause felt awkward. "Would you like to see the baby's things?" she asked. They were in a cedar chest right next to the empty crib, inches away from her bed. We sat together on the edge of her bed. She opened the cedar chest and one by one, brought out baby things and told me who had given or where she had gotten each blanket, sleeper, pair of booties. We touched and talked about the baby's things—and she thanked me so much for coming.

Ways to Convey Caring at First

    Expressing caring words
    Listening
    Touching
    Asking about how they are eating and sleeping
    Sending letters, cards, notes (keep them personal)
    Organizing meals to be brought in
    Returning medical supplies

Offering gifts of service. Be specific.
I'm available tomorrow afternoon to do some cleaning.
I'd be glad to keep both your kids this Saturday morning.
I'll come be company while you sort through his closet if you'd like.
I'll mow your lawn this weekend when I do mine.

Offer to phone the Social Security office, the kids' schools, an insurance agent, other calls needed.

Offer to do some home maintenance:
clean gutters, rake leaves, pull weeds, wash windows.

Do things which may be needed, such as checking the car, helping master the computer, accompanying to the cemetery.

Ways to Stay Caring Over Months
People fade after the first 2 - 4 weeks.
So keep sending notes, stop by, take food, call and offer to
stay and eat with them.
Offer to sit with them at church, programs, events.
Invite her on a hike or take her to breakfast.
Offer to go shopping with or for him.
Give the gift of a gardener or housekeeper for one day.

When Jack called I was sitting on the top basement step crying my eyes out and holding Ted's hunting boots—his old, dirty, worn hunting boots. I answered the phone and Jack said he was thinking about me and knew I'd be thinking about Ted. They'd gone hunting together every year for 20 some years. It was a loving, bittersweet, wonderful phone call at just the right moment in time.

Remember Important Dates

Anniversary dates of a death, a loved one's birthday, holidays, Mother's Day, Father's Day may be land-mined days. As the significant dates approach, tension rises. As one woman said, *The date is stalking me.* Part of grief support is being emotionally present at these predictably tender times.

Talk ahead of time about remembering the date.
The fear that no one will remember may be lonelier than the actual day.
Ask what they've thought about doing to honor that day.
We'll have more to say about this later.

Step Three
RESPECTING HOW ANOTHER GRIEVES

We each grieve in our own unique way. Our temperaments, family patterns and upbringing, cultural heritage and what we think people expect of us all influence how we show our grief. Some have by nature a more emotive or Affective style of grieving. Others have a more thinking or Cognitive style of grieving.

Some people are more Introverted and private. Others are Extroverted and very comfortable sharing feelings and details of their loss. Some of these styles are more frequently found among women and others more frequently among men. While style is influenced by gender it is not determined by it.

A person with an affective style is more likely to express strong feelings, tears, and a desire to talk about their experience. A person with a cognitive style may be less expressive of emotion. They are more likely to seek activity and thoughtful reflection in order to work through their grief.

Our role is to be respectful and accepting of what is healing for each of them. Grief support people are in the habit of asking about, as one man expressed it, *the F word—feelings, feelings, feelings.* For him, and other individuals with a more cognitive style, asking how he is doing may best be stated as:

What do you do with your sadness?
What do you do with your anger?
I know what it was like for me to sit with my mother when she was dying. What is it like for you to sit with your brother?
What helps you during such a chaotic time?

To ponder and discuss:

▸ What is my own style of grieving?

▸ What ways of grieving may be harder for me to recognize and support?

▸ What do I need to keep in mind when another person's grieving style is different from mine?

He had been best man in their wedding and his suicide had stunned everyone they knew. She had an urgent need to talk about it and she was frightened and hurt by her husband's silence. After the first couple of weeks he turned away whenever she brought it up. Didn't he care? He began running more than ever and began training for his first marathon. She was lonely and missed him when he was out running so much.

Only later did she understand that his running was his way of purging the grief. His 26-mile goal was countering his sense of helplessness and his running left him tired enough to finally sleep at night.

She joined a support group and talked her way through the pain. He ran until he could stand to stop running.

Step Four
Using Supportive Language

First of all, let's talk about phrases to avoid:

"At Least. . ."
A goal of grief support is to convey caring and give permission to grieve. Our job is to see that the words and phrases we use validate the loss and their right to be sad. Many common phrases do the opposite—they minimize the loss.

Notice what a message sounds like when it begins with *At least:*
At least you have other children.
At least he lived a full life.
At least he didn't suffer.
At least you're young (and can have more children, can get married again, etc.).
At least you got to know your baby before he died.
At least you didn't get to know your baby.
Notice how each one of these suggests the person who is grieving shouldn't be as sad as they are. So skip anything that starts with *At least . . .*

Sometimes a grieving person will say their own *At least . . .* This is their right. It's part of what gives them comfort. And it's very different when they say, *At least she isn't suffering any more,* or *I'm so grateful I still have one child to hold,* than when we try to get them to be grateful.

"God's Will. . ."
Be cautious with *God's will* and any phrase that suggests they should be more relieved or at peace than they are. Hear how painful it is rather than trying to convince them it's not. The convincing is for our benefit—to quiet our own sense of helplessness—rather than for theirs. Being company with them in their doubts and confusion will be more appreciated than trying to talk them into assurance.

When Helen's husband died, she sat by his bed in intensive care and said over and over, "It's God's will . . . it's God's will." His nurse simply stood beside her with a hand on her shoulder.

"How Are You?"
Another common difficulty for grieving people is to be asked over and over, day in and day out, *How are you?* It's an easy question to ask, but we give the grieving person the hard job of having to figure out an answer. *Fine* is a usual response to the question when it is a greeting—but clearly untrue in the midst of grief. As one young widower said, *"Fine"* is a four-letter word for me. *I feel as if I should have a "smile on a stick" to put in front of my mouth when I say it.*

Instead of *How are you?,* try a statement of caring:
I've been thinking of you. I know this has been a painful time.
I'm here for you. I'm wishing you some peaceful moments this weekend.

Clearly there are times when asking, *How are you?* and sitting down to invite heartfelt sharing is a gift, but it's wise to use the question sparingly and with an intention to listen.

Phrases of Judgment
Language both reveals and shapes our beliefs.
Think of the language that is often used to describe grieving:
• *Breaking down*
• *Losing it*
• *Falling apart*
• *Coming unglued*
• *Going to pieces*
Which of these sound like anything anyone ever ought to do?

Notice the difference in using the language of description:
• *Expressing grief*
• *Letting out powerful emotions*
• *Grieving*
• *Waves of sadness*
We can use language of description and invite the grieving person to do the same when he talks of times of intense sadness.

Offer honest words of caring. Share memories. Be available to listen and less eager to say the right thing. It's actually easier and more helpful.

Use the name of the one who has died. Ask what the bereaved remember most. Invite them to share photographs and stories.

Body Language
Our body language speaks as loudly as our words.
- Whenever possible be near eye level—sit or squat down when talking to a child or to someone in a chair or bed.
- When arms are free and uncrossed, it implies openness and invites more sharing.
- Using frequent eye contact conveys, *I'm here.*
- Sitting near suggests a willingness to stay put rather than flee.
- Three pats on the back may say, *There now, be done now,* while a hand on the shoulder or arm may invite continued talking.

TO PONDER AND DISCUSS:

▸ When I've been grieving, what did people say to me that did not help?

▸ What have people said when I was grieving that *did* feel caring?

▸ What am I prone to say that minimizes another's grief and what can I say more helpfully instead?

We were standing by the donuts at a meeting and a voice beside me said, "These are so sinful! I think I'll have two." I turned and there was one of my old friends who had just heard my son had died the month before. We looked at each other, our mouths dropped open and she said, "Kay! Oh Kay!" and grabbed me in a hug. Then she whispered, "I love you and now I'm gonna cry." So we both cried. She had called and written a note, but the simple words, "I love you and now I'm gonna cry," said it all.

Keeping Step Through Their Journey of Grief
Tending Your Own Grief

Before we can be there for someone else, we need to tend to our own losses. When we avoid our own sadness and confusion we're more likely to minimize or avoid the grief of others. That's because their grief mirrors the very things we are trying to avoid in ourselves.

We are all bereaved people. Loss comes in many forms. Death may be the most obvious loss but not the only one that shakes up and re-arranges our lives. Loss of a significant relationship, loss of health, hopes and dreams, familiar work, possessions, beloved pets are all losses we know only too well. It's risky to care and to love. But it's profoundly lonely to refuse to care or love.

There is a wealth of printed material designed to be company in the exploring of a loss. Friends, counselors, support groups, quiet reflective time, rituals and creative projects are all ways to move through a stuck place. Doing your own healing work will allow you to be much more present and attentive to the grief needs of those you meet.

TO PONDER AND DISCUSS:

‣ What are the significant losses of my life?

‣ What are the ones I anticipate or fear?

‣ What have I done that has helped me make peace with a loss?

‣ What would still be helpful for me to do?

When I was meeting with a man whose brother had died in a car wreck, I realized I was becoming more and more preoccupied with memories of my own sister's death. She had also died in a car wreck when she was in high school years before. I could suddenly and vividly picture the police at the door, the wake, the gloom in the house the rest of my senior year. I was having a hard time really hearing this man.

That weekend I went for a long hike. I told my sister I missed her still; told her how helpless I had felt as her big brother. Before the hike was over I knew I had a gift from her—a gift of compassion that would help me reach out to others.

Hearing the Story

There is healing in telling the story. The willingness to listen, over and over if needed, invites the telling.

But grieving people soon discover most don't want to hear their stories. Friends and family want them to be over it and presume telling just makes it hurt more. For those who would like to share what has happened, a willing listener is a wonderful gift.

Sit with them, be informal and inviting. Resist the urge to relate your or another's story. Simply be present and available. Listen to their experience with an open heart.

Some open questions that invite sharing might be:
- *How and where did you hear the news?*
- *What was your first reaction?*
- *Who was there for support? Who wasn't there?*
- *What was hardest?*
- *What memories are most special? Most troubling?*
- *What dates will be most significant this year?*

And the simple invitation, *Tell me about it.*

In hearing you will learn much about what this loss means and how it impacts the person's life.

What is the meaning of this loss?

We rarely minimize a loss when we understand it's meaning. Loss means change. It may be helpful to ponder and reflect with them:

- *What have you lost?*
- *What does it mean to you that this has happened?*
- *How is life different now?*
- *How are you different?*
- *What beliefs or fears are you struggling with?*

Explore what feels unfinished.

- *Did you say a goodbye?*
- *Did you hear a goodbye (literally or symbolically)?*
- *What do you wish you could have done or said?*
- *What do you wish you could have heard?*
- *Did you have the opportunity to participate in closure rituals?*
- *What do you need or what do you want to do now?*

What gifts remain?

When a loved one dies, the bonds of closeness remain beyond death. Grieving people may feel pressed by those around them to "let go" and to "move on with their lives." But relationships bring gifts to keep always. Recognizing this may offer some comfort.

You might ask:

- *What gift of the heart from this person will you always keep?*
- *What message or gift would they give you now if they could?*
- *What token of their love or comfort can you keep near you?*

Who and what is supporting and sustaining them now?

Be willing to hear how faith or God is of great comfort now. Be willing to hear when their faith is shaken and is part of the loss. Support may be very different from what you imagine. Stroking the cat or listening to soft music may be their moment of solace. Comfort may come through nature or solitude or hugs from friends.

She was just a little dog, but when my husband died she read my emotions and stuck close by me in my grief. When I wept she jumped up on my lap, at times licking my tears. She curled up with me for hours while I napped. When it was time to get up she begged for a walk and showed me how to play. She was my solace, my support.

Exploring Ways of Releasing Grief

When there was no goodbye, when something important was not said or heard, there are ways to complete the interrupted message. As one person put it, *Unfinished business is about undelivered messages.* Is there a message he wishes he could give or receive? Can he imagine a way to still do that?

SPEAKING OR WRITING TO THE PERSON
Have you ever been in a meeting or gathering and not liked the way it went? Did you find yourself finishing your speech in the car on the way home? And didn't it help even though no one was there to hear it? That's an example of *having your say.*

Speaking aloud, with or without company, or writing a message as if in a letter are ways of having your say. Some ways to begin may be:
>*What I need you to hear is . . .*
>*I regret . . .*
>*I resent . . .*
>*I'm sad . . .*
>*I miss . . .*
>*I'm angry . . .*
>*I appreciate . . .*
>*I want to thank you for . . .*
>*I will always remember . . .*

SPEAKING OR WRITING FROM THE PERSON
Ask what needs to be heard from the person who died.
Is it a goodbye, words of regret or affirmation?
Permission or forgiveness?
Encourage writing it out or speaking it as the other would have.
Let *them* have their say.

SPECIFIC DAILY OR WEEKLY GRIEF TIME

Sometimes embracing the experience of grief is scary. Trying not to think about it is a common way to try to avoid pain. But too often it's like having one foot on the brake and one on the accelerator. We don't make any progress but it tears up the engine. Grieving people need a way to release what is churning inside that feels safe and contained.

You could even say trying not to grieve is like trying to dam up a rising river. Sooner or later it will overflow. A grieving person may feel more in control by opening a flood gate at appointed times and letting some of the pressure out. Even though the river will continue to rise, there is now a little leeway.

The purpose of a specific daily or weekly grief time is to build in time to express grief while still maintaining some sense of control.
• Make an appointment with Grief.
• Schedule blocks of time (try 45 minutes) and literally set a timer.
• Make it private time without any interruptions.
• Gather pictures, letters, powerful reminders of the one who has died.
• Speak out loud or contemplate or weep or hold the reminders.
• Be with whatever comes. If feelings are intense, let them flow.
• If you feel numb, simply be with the numbness.
• When the timer rings say, *I'm going to go for now* and *I'll be back . . .* (identify when).
• Put the things away. The folding or packing away helps with transition.
• Have a pre-planned activity to do next.

The grief times may be daily, every other day, twice a week, weekly. Gradually they can be spaced farther apart to fit the need. Later they may be reserved for anniversary dates. This is permission to grieve and yet within boundaries to offer some emotional safety. Obviously grief isn't tidy or tame. Strong feelings will still come at other times. It may, however, become easier to bracket the feelings and tend to them at intentional times.

Honoring Key Dates

Few of us have had much guidance about what to do on the key dates following a loss. Keeping busy on that day is a strategy that rarely works and usually adds to the isolation.

Key dates may include:
• Anniversary of the death or diagnosis
• Birthday
• Wedding anniversary
• Engagement anniversary
• Due date when it's a pregnancy loss
• Holidays
• What would have been graduation day
• All those private but significant dates on the calendar of the heart

We decided to acknowledge the obvious. We all missed Mom, so at our holiday table we placed flowers on her plate. It was very comforting.

Ask what a person has thought about doing on that day. They may have an idea but are afraid to act on it for fear it sounds strange. Assure them that myriads of things have been done, privately and publicly, on significant dates. Since there's no guidance there are also no shoulds.

Some possibilities include:
• Lighting a candle and letting it burn in a safe place for the day
• Taking flowers to the grave
• Fixing the favorite food of the person who died
• Hiking to a special place
• Getting a massage
• Spending the day with a friend
• Writing in a journal
• Playing a piece of music in their honor
• Mailing yourself a beautiful card

To ponder and discuss:

▸ What are things I have done on a key date to honor a loss?

▸ What are things I have heard of others doing?

It was a very simple thing to do. Dad had always carved the turkey on Thanksgiving, so I tied a yellow ribbon around the carving knife, lit a candle on the table and told everyone they were both in memory of Dad.

Welcoming Joyful Moments

I will always remember the gift of a client who said what helped her through a difficult year was waking each morning and saying aloud, *Today I welcome a moment of joy.* She made a point of watching for it each day and writing it on the calendar. The moment of joy might have been a call from a friend, a hug, a brief burst of sunshine, the smell of the bakery on the way to work, overhearing a piece of music, a sunset.

The very act of watching for them opened her to be receptive and she found she took in all kinds of joyful and encouraging moments that otherwise she would have missed. Later, looking back over the calendar of that year, she was amazed at what a difference those moments had made.

If joy is too exuberant a word in the midst of grief it may be possible to simply say, *Today I welcome a moment of comfort,* or *Today I welcome a moment of peace.* And being the practical sort, I suggest that if it hasn't found you by four o'clock in the afternoon, pick up the phone and help it along.

Keeping Yourself Refilled

Refilling Is the Key to Giving

Meeting with people who are grieving takes energy and stamina. Our caring is a huge gift. And how much can we give to others without refilling before we give out? Refilling is our key to giving. We need to refill our own pitcher before we can refill the glasses of others.

Where is your emotional fuel level right now? How refilled or close to empty have you averaged over the past three or four months? Assessing where you are is an important step in creating a plan for keeping refilled. Are you above two-thirds full? Under the half-way mark? Down to eighth of a tank? Running on fumes? One woman told me, *I'm past fumes—I've been pushing the car uphill for the past two weeks and it just rolled over me!* Now that's a bit beyond depleted!

What are your early signs of depletion? There are many possible early warning signs. It may be apathy, or irritability, or insomnia, or forgetting appointments, or low energy, or a general sense that you aren't enjoying your work or your life. If you have shame about getting depleted, as I used to have, it will be easy to deny or overlook these signals. But depletion will get your attention sooner or later. Paying attention to early signs allows you to take corrective action while it is still relatively easy to do.

What choices do you make that deplete you? We're not asking what do other people do that contribute to your being weary, but what do *you* do? The distinction is crucial. You see, if I'm blaming others for my depletion, then I have to get others to change before I can be refilled—and that's a sure prescription for discouragement. But as soon as I recognize that my choices deplete or refill me, change is within my reach.

Choices that deplete may be as ordinary as not getting enough sleep or disregarding your personal needs for exercise and healthy nutrition. A fast way to depletion is saying yes to more than you can do without exhaustion or resentment. If you struggle with automatic yes-saying, put a moratorium on any new yes's until you've paused a few minutes or slept on it overnight. Check your fuel gauge. Ask yourself, Can I say yes without resentment? Resentment is a wise and useful guide. The pausing will give you time to write and practice your words if you decide to say no.

Learning to Say No Without Over Explaining and Without Guilt

So often the desire to please others and receive their approval drives us to say yes when we know it's time to say no. One person described this very well: *When I say no, I die of guilt; when I say yes, I die of resentment.* But overspending our time and energy is no more responsible than overspending financially. Learning to say no is healthy boundary setting. Healthy boundary setting allows us to preserve energy for what we value most.

Practice language of choice. Instead of, *"I'm sorry but I can't possibly,"* try, *"I've thought about that and have decided to decline this time."* Or, *"That doesn't work at all for me this week."* Period. You don't owe an explanation. Work up to modeling healthy boundary setting instead of sneaking it: *"I've decided to keep this Saturday free for refilling."*

Refilling is healthy self care.
It's getting depleted that is selfish because then I have nothing to give.

Learning to Play Even When the Work Is Not Done

Most of us grew up with the old adage about finishing our work before play. That made sense when we had three, ten-minute jobs for the day! But we grew out of that place years ago. Non-stop work guarantees we'll become depleted.

Federal law gives production workers a fifteen-minute break every four hours. Businesses know productivity is higher and there is less time off for accidents when workers take breaks. If you are your own boss, consider getting into compliance. Learn to stop and relax and play. *Make enjoying your day as high a priority as the work you accomplish.*

TO PONDER AND DISCUSS:

▸ How depleted or refilled am I right now?

▸ What are my early signs of depletion?

▸ What choices do I make that lead to my getting depleted?

One day I realized I was furious at the house plants because they needed water again from me! Well, that got my attention. It was so absurd I actually chuckled. It was the first time it hit me how empty I felt. I arranged for a long weekend and went to the coast.

What Refills You?

What fills you up and delights your heart? Identify those things that take little energy. List those that take more energy.

> Listening to or playing music
> Journaling
> Holding a warm mug in your hands
> Calling a friend out of town
> Planning an outing by yourself
> Visiting a friend
> Soaking in the tub
> Blowing bubbles
> Hiking with a friend
> Creative projects
> Taking a vacation
> Taking a fun class
> Enjoying chocolate

Tending the garden
Petting a puppy
Eating a good lunch
Playing
Licking an ice cream cone
Participating in a fiercely competitive sport
Fishing
Having something gift wrapped—when it's for you
Tending to your spirituality

Keeping refilled means learning to say yes to what you delight in. Replenishing is about being kind, affirming and generous to yourself.

Think of a river, and remember you can give as much as you are willing to receive.

To ponder and discuss:

▸ What are some of my favorite ways of refilling?

▸ What am I ready to commit to that will help refill me?

Summing It Up

Being with grieving people is awkward because we feel helpless, we are reminded of our own losses and we may have had little guidance.

There are *Four Guiding Steps* for how to be supportive.

Step One: Learn the art of *being* rather than *doing*. There is nothing we can do to take away another's grief. Our job is to let go of trying to fix pain, learn to tolerate our own sense of helplessness and trust their healing process. What we can add is the memory of our caring.

Step Two: Acknowledge the obvious. Avoid avoiding. Reach out and let them know you are aware and thinking of them.

Step Three: Respect how another grieves, whether it be more Affective or Cognitive, more Introverted or Extroverted, similar or dissimilar to your own grieving style.

Step Four: Use supportive language to validate rather than minimize the loss. Avoid *At least*; be careful of *God's will* messages. Offer caring statements rather than automatically asking, *How are you?* Be present and inviting with words and body language.

Tend to your own griefwork as a prerequisite for supporting others.

Be open to hearing their story, and be company through their long journey of grief.

Listen for what may have been left unfinished.

Explore ways of releasing grief.
Some ways to encourage this include:
- Having one's say by speaking or writing to and/or from the person who is gone
- Creating daily or weekly grief time
- Honoring key dates
- Welcoming joyful or comforting moments

Keep yourself refilled.
- Check your fuel gauge and learn your early signs of depletion.
- Learn to say no without overexplaining and without guilt.
- Learn to play even though the work isn't done.
- Learn to say yes to what delights you.

The Last Step

Your commitment to being supportive to others in their grief is a compassionate gift. Go with courage and a willingness to learn from those who grieve. They have always been and will always be our most memorable teachers. Go with a willingness to learn about yourself. Go with a willingness to wear your times of helplessness and your times of quiet joy.

Names and Dates to Remember

Important Notes

About the Author

 Marilyn Gryte is a Licensed Professional Counselor with a clinical practice in Albany, Oregon. She has taught a graduate grief counseling class for Oregon State University, traveled nationally with grief education seminars and has a background in nursing and childbearing loss support.

In addition to **Stepping Through the Awkwardness,** Marilyn has written **No New Baby,** for children whose baby sister or brother dies before birth and **Inner Healing After Ending A Pregnancy.**

For other resources on grief and loss contact

Centering Corporation
P.O. Box 4600
Omaha NE 68104

Phone: 402-553-1200
Fax: 402-553-0507